The Code and Cipher Book

The Code & Cipher book

By JANE SARNOFF and REYNOLD RUFFINS

Text copyright © 1975 Jane Sarnoff/Illustrations copyright © 1975 Reynold Ruffins/Copyright under the Berne Convention/All rights reserved.
Printed in the United States of America/Library of Congress Catalog Card Number 74-24419/ISBN-0-684-14246-5
1 3 5 7 9 11 13 15 17 19 RD/C 20 18 16 14 12 10 8 6 4 2

Charles Scribner's Sons
New York

Dedicated to

The **Code and Cipher Book** can help you keep almost anything and everything secret. There are over twenty-five different ways to write, speak, flash, whistle, whittle, and even embroider secret messages. Also included are hints for making up your own codes and ciphers, devices for encoding (putting into code) and decoding (taking out of code), recipes for invisible ink, methods of inkless writing, information about breaking codes, facts about codes in history, practice riddles in code…and more.

There are really only two basic ways to write secret messages—codes and ciphers. In a code, each real word has another word to stand for it. Green, for example, could be a code word for hello. Blue could be a code word for friend. A greeting would be "Green, blue."

In ciphers, letters rather than words are changed. Most of the time when people talk about codes they really mean ciphers. Sometimes, in this book, the word code is used to mean cipher.

There are two different types of ciphers—transposition ciphers and substitution ciphers. In a transposition cipher, all the letters of the message stay the same—just their order is changed. In a substitution cipher the order of the letters stays the same, but each letter is replaced by something else. The substitute could be another letter, a number, a symbol, or a picture.

The Code and Cipher Book will help you pass a secret on and still keep it secret. And by the way, green, blue.

1 Space Cipher

| the message is: **I HAVE TEN CHOCOLATE COOKIES.** |

One of the easiest ways to encode a message is to take out or change the space between words. In Space Cipher the message is written:

IHA VETE NCH OCOLA TECO OKIES

The letters are divided into groups of three, four, and five letters to make the message harder to break. Be sure your partner knows the cipher you are using.

2 Backward Cipher

| the message is: **HOW CAN WE DIVIDE TEN BY THREE?** |

Writing a message backward is another way of encoding it. In Backward Cipher the message is written:

EERHT YB NET EDIVID EW NAC WOH

Never use punctuation marks in coded messages; they make the messages easier to break.

3 Space and Backward Ciphers Combined

| the message is: **DO NOT TELL SETH WE HAVE THE COOKIES.** |

Both the Space Cipher and the Backward Cipher can be broken by someone who is used to codes. But, if you put a message into Space Cipher and then into Backward Cipher, it becomes much harder to break. The message, when both ciphers are used, is written:

SEIKO OCEH TEVA HEWH TESL LETT ONOD

---

encode this: THESE COOKIES ARE TERRIBLE.

decode this: SELBM URCE IKOO CEHTY AWE HTST AHT

Something not to write in Backward Cipher: Too hot to hoot.

Redivider is one of the longest words in English that is the same backward as forward.

When a message is not encoded or enciphered it is called the "plain text."

4 Picket Fence Cipher

Count the number of letters in the message. If the number cannot be divided by two, add a dummy letter to the end of the message.

Write the message on two lines with every other letter on the lower line. Do not leave any space between words. The message will look like the top of a picket fence.

I I P D Y W A E O T A P C E F N E
R P E M S E T R N H T I K T E C K *dummy letter*

Write the top line of letters, followed by the bottom line.

IIPDYWAEOTAPCEFNERPEMSETRNHTIKTECK

To make the message even harder to break, but easier to encode and decode, divide the message into letter groups of three, four, or five letters.

IIPDY WAEOT APCEF NERP EMSET RNHT IKT ECK

To decode a message written in the Picket Fence Cipher, divide the message exactly in half. Take the first letter of the left half and follow it with the first letter of the right half. Next comes the second letter from the left half followed by the second letter from the right half. Continue until all the letters are in order. Ignore the dummy letter at the end. You will have to figure out where the spaces go between words.

---

encode this: WHY DID YOU WEAR A SWEATER?

decode this: BCUE YOHR ACLE ASM MTE WSOD

Dummy letters, numbers, or symbols are called "nulls."

The word cryptology comes from two Greek words—kryptos (secret or hidden) and graphos (writing).

All enciphering should be done on a single sheet of paper on top of a hard plastic or glass table so that no impression will remain after the message has been written.

5 Maze Cipher

the message is: **THE PASSWORD FOR TODAY IS PEANUTS.**

A Maze Cipher is really a more complicated kind of Picket Fence Cipher—in both, the letters of the message are scrambled up. To encode a message in a Maze Cipher, first count the number of letters in the message, then add dummy letters to make the number come out to a multiple of five. Here the number of letters is twenty-eight. **K** and **X** have been added to make the message number thirty. Draw a grid of six rows of five boxes each. Write the message inside the grid, one letter to a box. Start at the upper left box and fill in the rows from left to right. The message would be written:

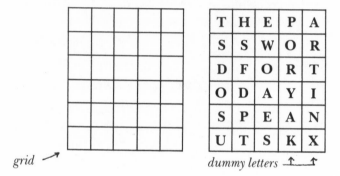

grid

T	H	E	P	A
S	S	W	O	R
D	F	O	R	T
O	D	A	Y	I
S	P	E	A	N
U	T	S	K	X

dummy letters

There are many different pathways you can use to scramble your message. Choose a pathway and write the message, all on one line, by following the line of the pathway through the message. After you have encoded the message, divide the letters into groups of three, four, or five.

PEANUTS

T	H	E	P	A
S	S	W	O	R
D	F	O	R	T
O	D	A	Y	I
S	P	E	A	N
U	T	S	K	X

pathway **1.**

T	H	E	P	A
S	S	W	O	R
D	F	O	R	T
O	D	A	Y	I
S	P	E	A	N
U	T	S	K	X

pathway **2.**

T	H	E	P	A
S	S	W	O	R
D	F	O	R	T
O	D	A	Y	I
S	P	E	A	N
U	T	S	K	X

pathway **3.**

T	H	E	P	A
S	S	W	O	R
D	F	O	R	T
O	D	A	Y	I
S	P	E	A	N
U	T	S	K	X

pathway **4.**

The same message is written differently when different pathways are used.

1. TSDO SUT PDFSH EWOA ESKAY ROPA RTINX   **3.** THSD SEP WFOSD OOAR RAPUT EYTI ASKNX

2. APEH TSS WORTR OFDO DAYIN AEPS UTSKX   **4.** USOD STH EPART INXK STPDF SWOR YAEAO

To decode a message sent in a Maze Cipher you need to know the number of rows and columns in the grid and the pathway that was used to encode the message. Draw an empty grid with the right number of rows and columns. Put the first letter of the message at the starting point of the pathway. Continue to put the letters in the grid, following the pathway. The message can be read by following each row from left to right, starting at the top and finishing at the bottom.

---

encode this: ELEPHANTS EAT THE SHELLS TOO. *(use a few different pathways)*

decode this: IPFA RGODS TAATL HSSOD MWEL EUOP OMX *(grid size: 6x5, pathway 1)*

If you and your partner want to get really confusing, there are a number of different changes you can make in the Maze Cipher.

1. Change the way in which you write the message in the grid—let the message read from right to left, or down to up, or both.

2. Change the number of rows, or the number of columns, or both. The empty grid should have at least as many spaces as the message, but you can add a lot of dummy letters.

3. Dummy letters don't have to go at the end of the message. Agree with your partner that every fourth or fifth square in the grid is a dummy letter. Try adding dummy numbers to make the message look really confusing.

No matter what changes you make in the basic Maze, be sure that you and your partner agree on the method to be used.

6 Alphabet Shift Cipher

Write the alphabet across the page, all on one line. This is your real alphabet. To work out your cipher alphabet, choose a key number—any number from one to twenty-five. The key number here is three.

Starting with **B**, count three letters to the right. You will end on **D**. Put **A** of the cipher alphabet above the **D** of the real alphabet. Continue writing out the cipher alphabet until you reach the real **Z**. Then go back to the real **A** and continue with the cipher alphabet until you reach the cipher **Z**. Every real letter should have a cipher letter above it.

cipher: X Y Z A B C D E F G H I J K L M N O P Q R S T U V W
real: A B C D E F G H I J K L M N O P Q R S T U V W X Y Z

You are now ready to send and receive messages in the Alphabet Shift Cipher.

encode this: WHAT IS THE GOLDEN RULE?
decode this: TELBSBO CFKAP DLIA CFOPQ HBBMP FQ

You can change the cipher alphabet just by changing the key number. If your key number is five, start with the real **B** and count over five letters. Put the cipher **A** above the real **F** and finish the cipher alphabet.

A code word can be used to tell your partner the key number for decoding a message. "Octopus" would mean that the key number is seven—the number of letters in the word, *not* the number of arms on the octopus. Since seven is the key number, the cipher **A** should go above the real **H**.

Alphabet Shift Ciphers are sometimes called Caesar Ciphers because Julius Caesar used one. His key number was usually three.

In 1587, Mary Queen of Scots was plotting to assassinate Queen Elizabeth I of England and seize her throne. Mary sent letters about the plot, in secret cipher, to a friend. The letters were captured by the chief of Elizabeth's spy service. The cipher Mary used was too easy to decode…and Mary lost her head.

The most important rule of secret writing: a secret message must be safe enough so that by the time the enemy solves it, it is too late to be of any use.

In Elizabethan times, shorthand wasn't used by secretaries, it was used by spies as a type of secret writing. Shorthand ciphers were used by the Greeks as early as 195 A.D.

Newspapers were used in England, many years ago, to send secret messages. The sender spelled out the message with a pin prick or a dot under certain letters or words.

7 Key Word Shift Cipher

As with the regular Alphabet Shift Cipher, write the alphabet across the page, all on one line. This is your real alphabet. Choose a key word. Here the key word is "stupid." Above the real alphabet write stupid followed by all the other letters of the alphabet, leaving out the letters in stupid.

cipher: S T U P I D A B C E F G H J K L M N O Q R V W X Y Z
real: A B C D E F G H I J K L M N O P Q R S T U V W X Y Z

Because stupid has no letter in the alphabet after U, the last five letters are the same in the real alphabet and the cipher alphabet. It is a good idea to choose a word with letters as far back in the alphabet as possible so that not too many of the cipher and the real letters are the same. If there is a Y in your key word the only letters that will be the same are the Z's. Your key word should be as long as possible, but should not repeat any letters. Change your key word from time to time so that anyone trying to break your cipher will get confused.

encode this: I BEAT MY BROTHER UP EVERY MORNING.
decode this: C AIQ RL SQ OIVIJ SJP BI AIQO RL SQ ICABQ

8 Backward Alphabet Cipher

Write the alphabet across the page. Above it, but starting with Z and continuing backward, write the cipher alphabet.

cipher: Z Y X W V U T S R Q P O N M L K J I H G F E D C B A
real: A B C D E F G H I J K L M N O P Q R S T U V W X Y Z

The Backward Alphabet Cipher is a good cipher to use with other ciphers. Try combining a Space Cipher and the Backward Alphabet Cipher. Add dummy letters for extra confusion. As always, be sure your partner knows the codes you are using.

encode this: YOU ARE SUPPOSED TO EAT A BALANCED MEAL.
decode this: VEVIB KRVXV LU XZMWB DVRTSH GSV HZNV

9 Backward Shift Cipher

You can make a Backward Shift Cipher just the way you did the Alphabet Shift Cipher. First write out the real alphabet, then choose a key number. Here the key number is four. Start with **B** in the real alphabet and count over four. Above the real **E**, put the cipher **Z** and continue writing the cipher alphabet backward.

cipher: D C B A Z Y X W V U T S R Q P O N M L K J I H G F E
real: A B C D E F G H I J K L M N O P Q R S T U V W X Y Z

To decode a message in a Backward Shift Cipher you need to know the key number…and the backward part.

encode this: CHANGE THE CODE AT MIDNIGHT. *(use five as the key number)*
decode this: Y AS NS FCD GN TYTC *(seven is the key number)*

In the Middle Ages, most people couldn't read or write. A prince could send a pageboy with a message in plain text to a noble lady and be sure that it could not be read any better than the most complicated code.

Codes and ciphers were supposed to be used only by royalty or by people in the service of royalty. Other people could be beheaded if caught using ciphers or codes.

Prisoners in early England used a tapping cipher. Tapping messages on the walls of the dungeons took a long time—but the prisoners had plenty of time. The prisoners divided the alphabet into five groups of letters:

The number of the group was tapped first and then the position of the letter in the group. To tap O, the prisoner would first tap three times, to stand for the group of letters, and then tap four times to stand for the fourth letter in that group.

ABCDE FGH*I*/*J*K LMNOP QRSTU VWXYZ

Diplomats and ambassadors have always liked invisible inks better than codes or ciphers. With invisible inks no one even knows a message has been sent.

During the Middle Ages, picture ciphers using the signs of the Zodiac were very popular.

Ship captains of the navy bound their codebooks in lead. If it looked like the enemy was going to win a battle, the codebooks were thrown overboard to sink.

10 Number Cipher

Write the alphabet across the page, all on one line. Above the **A**, put a **1**. Above the **B**, put a **2**. Go straight to the end of the alphabet. Above the **Z** will be a **26.** When you encode a message, put a dash between each number or the receiver won't know if **11** is two **A**'s in a row or one **K**.

cipher:	1	2	3	4	5	6	7	8	9	10	11	12	13	14	15	16	17	18	19	20	21	22	23	24	25	26
real:	A	B	C	D	E	F	G	H	I	J	K	L	M	N	O	P	Q	R	S	T	U	V	W	X	Y	Z

encode this: YOUR DAYS ARE NUMBERED.

decode this: 3-15-21-14-20 20-15 20-5-14

11 Number Shift Cipher

Write the alphabet across the page, all on one line. Choose a key number and make that number equal to **A.** Write the key number above **A** and finish the alphabet from that number. When the key number is **8,** the cipher looks like this:

cipher:	8	9	10	11	12	13	14	15	16	17	18	19	20	21	22	23	24	25	26	27	28	29	30	31	32	33
real:	A	B	C	D	E	F	G	H	I	J	K	L	M	N	O	P	Q	R	S	T	U	V	W	X	Y	Z

To tell your partner what the key number is, choose a secret word and let the number of letters in the word be the key number. Or, use the date of your birthday. If your birthday were November 8, you would take the 8 and add 11 to it because November is the eleventh month. Your key number would be 19. Just make sure your partner knows your birthday.

encode this: HOW OLD WILL RICHARD BE NEXT YEAR? *(use 17 as the key number)*

decode this: 22-21-12 32-12-8-25 22-19-11-12-25 *(8 is the key number)*

The order of the numbers in the cipher alphabet can be mixed up to make number ciphers harder to break. Both sender and receiver then need a key to encode and decode.

Twenty-six numbers can be arranged in 17,534,411,353,330,679,808,000,000 different ways.

12 Grid Number Cipher

Draw a grid that has five squares across and five squares down. On the outside of the grid, number the squares across (column numbers) and the squares down (row numbers). Put one letter of the alphabet in each square. Since five times five is twenty-five and there are twenty-six letters in the alphabet, two letters have to share one square. Here **Y** and **Z** share a square since zou won't mix them up in a message.

	1	2	3	4	5
1	A	B	C	D	E
2	F	G	H	I	J
3	K	L	M	N	O
4	P	Q	R	S	T
5	U	V	W	X	Y/Z

The key to the cipher is made up by writing a letter's row number followed by its column number. Each letter has two numbers: **A** is **1** (the row number) and **1** (the column number), written as **11**. **B** is **12**, **C** is **13**, **D** is **14**, and on through the alphabet.

After a message has been enciphered, divide the numbers into groups of five. Since each letter has been replaced by two numbers, it is not hard to redivide the numbers for decoding...unless the decoder doesn't know the method.

"Hungry Dogs" first looks like this: **23 51 34 22 43 55/ 14 35 22 44**. When the numbers are divided into groups of five it looks like this: **23513 42243 55143 52244**.

---

encode this: HOT DOGS NEED MUSTARD.

decode this: **13353 21414 35224 43415 15144 11134 45440** *(0 is a dummy number)*

The Grid Number Cipher was first devised by Polybius, a writer in ancient Greece.

A decoded message is called "cleared".

BURR FARMS SCHOOL
WESTPORT, CONN.

13 Porta's Simple Cipher Table

In 1563, an Italian magician and scientist, Giovanni Porta, published a book of codes that included a cipher table that had 676 strange symbols to substitute for pairs of letters. Here is an easy form of Porta's Cipher Table—it uses only five different alphabet arrangements.

1. A B C D E F G H I J K L M
   N O P Q R S T U V W X Y Z

2. A B C D E F G H I J K L M
   Z N O P Q R S T U V W X Y

3. A B C D E F G H I J K L M
   Y Z N O P Q R S T U V W X

4. A B C D E F G H I J K L M
   X Y Z N O P Q R S T U V W

5. A B C D E F G H I J K L M
   W X Y Z N O P Q R S T U V

Each alphabet arrangement has been divided in half. To encipher a letter, find it and take the letter opposite it. In the first alphabet, for example: **A** is **N** and **N** is **A**. In the second alphabet, **A** is **Z** and **Z** is **A**. And so on.

If there are five words in your message, encipher the first word from the first alphabet, the second word from the second alphabet...If there are more than five words, just start over again with the first alphabet for the sixth word.

You will need to carry the Porta Table with you for coding and decoding, but it is just the right size for copying on a file card. If you think someone has copied your table and you don't have time to make a new one by changing the alphabet arrangements, just change the order of the use of the alphabets. For example, the first word could be enciphered from the fifth alphabet, the second word from the fourth alphabet, and on up the list. Just make sure your partner knows the order of the alphabets.

encode this: WANT TO HAVE A MAGIC SHOW? *(alphabet order 1,3,4,5,2)*
decode this: LRF MCI NYC YO KQN ENOOVG *(alphabet order regular)*

14 A Modern/Ancient Cipher

The Ancient Ogam Cipher Before the year one, in what is now England, the ruling people were the Celts. The Celts invented a symbol substitution cipher of straight lines called ogams. Some of the ogam writing might have been used for everyday messages—Ye olde cakes are cooking—but some messages were carved on stone monuments that are still standing today.

The Roman alphabet, which the Celts used, has most, but not all, of the letters of our alphabet.

The Modern Ogam Cipher The Celts' method of using different kinds of straight lines above and below a center line makes a good cipher with our alphabet today. To make the Ogam Cipher more modern and easier to encode and decode, the cipher has been put in alphabetical order and the groups of five lines have been written ||||| .

Try whittling an Ogam message on an old board.

---

encode this: I HATE EYE OF NEWT.

decode this:

The work of archaeologists often seems a lot like code breaking. They have to figure out the mysterious writings ancient peoples left on tombs and tablets.

15 Tic Tac Toe Cipher

Draw a large tic tac toe board. Put three letters, one under the other, in every space. The last space will have only **Y** and **Z**. The "extra" place in that space can be used for a question mark.

A	J	S
B	K	T
C	L	U
D	M	V
E	N	W
F	O	X
G	P	Y
H	Q	Z
I	R	?

The cipher key is made up of a combination of lines—to show the right space—and a dot—to show the position of the letter in the space. Each cipher letter is a picture of the space a letter is in. For the letter **N** in this cipher, draw a square to show that the letter is in the center space and then put a dot in the middle of the square to show that the **N** is the middle letter of the square.

cipher:
real: A B C D E F G H I J K L M N O P Q R S T U V W X Y Z ?

---

encode this: DOES YOUR FATHER BELIEVE IN CLUBS FOR KIDS?

decode this:

You can change the whole Tic Tac Toe Cipher just by changing the order of the letters on the tic tac toe board from up and down to side by side.

ABC	DEF	GHI
JKL	MNO	PQR
STU	VWX	YZ?

16 Pigpen Cipher

Draw a tic tac toe board, a large X, and then draw another set. Put a dot in each space in the last set. If you count the spaces you will find that there are twenty-six—just the number of letters in the alphabet. Put one letter in each space.

A	B	C
D	E	F
G	H	I

L
K M
J

N	O	P
Q	R	S
T	U	V

Y
X Z
W

A message is encoded in the Pigpen Cipher by substituting a drawing of the space a letter is in for the letter itself.

encode this: WHAT IS PIGSKIN USED FOR?

decode this:

You can change the key to the Pigpen Cipher just by changing the order of the letters in the spaces. Or, put the dots in the first half of the alphabet. As always, be sure your partner knows what you are doing.

Tic Tac Toe and Pigpen are easy ciphers to embroider. Stitch a secret message or your name on blue jeans, tee shirt, or jacket. And what about a club flag?

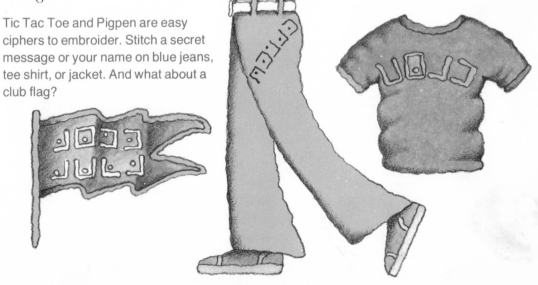

The people who live in a part of London where the Bow Bell can be heard are called Cockneys. They have two code languages. One is a rhyming slang which started centuries ago as a secret code of thieves who lived in the area. In the Rhyming Slang a phrase, the last word of which rhymes with the real word, is substituted for the real word.

Cockneys also speak in Back Slang. The words are spelled backward (in the speaker's mind) and then pronounced in the easiest way possible. Sometimes the words get extra letters put in. Back Slang itself is _Kabec Genals._

Cockneys mix up Rhyming Slang and Back Slang to make a third code language called Center Slang.

Church—lean and lurch

Home—top of Rome

Eyes—meat pies

Dance—kick and prance

Drunk—Jumbo's trunk

Whiskey—gay and frisk

Drink—tumble down the sink

Tea—Rosy Lee

Stairs—apples and pears

Kids—God forbids

Knees—bread and cheese

Center Slang
God forbids, teg ruoy German bands ffo ym jack dandy
ro ym plates of meat lliw pots uoy.

Cop—ginger pop

17 Letter/Word Cipher

Each letter of the alphabet, instead of being replaced by another letter, number, or symbol, can be replaced by a word or phrase. You can make up your own Letter/Word Cipher, or use this one.

A	spaghetti		**N**	potato chips
B	raisins		**O**	pizza
C	ice cream		**P**	chocolate chips
D	gum drops		**Q**	soda pop
E	hot fudge		**R**	candy bar
F	sprinkles		**S**	apple pie
G	banana split		**T**	birthday cake
H	taffy		**U**	chewing gum
I	hot dogs		**V**	strawberry shortcake
J	mustard		**W**	gingerbread
K	ketchup		**X**	whipped cream
L	hamburgers		**Y**	brownies
M	dill pickles		**Z**	beets

A message in this code would take a long time to write, but it would look like the world's best shopping list.

encode this: SNACK TIME.

decode this: TAFFY CHEWING GUM POTATO CHIPS BANANA SPLIT CANDY BAR BROWNIES

24

18 Typewriter Random Cipher

The word random means "without plan." To make a random cipher, write out the letters of the alphabet, and above each letter put a symbol—a letter, number, or picture. There should be no order or plan in the way the symbols are arranged. A random cipher is harder to break than a planned cipher, but, since the keys to the random ciphers are hard to remember, you usually have to carry a key with you.

This random cipher uses punctuation marks and other symbols that are found on a typewriter.

cipher:	.	%	*	#	?	"	¼	0	−	=	¢	&	'	/	!	@	x	(	;	,	)	½	$	6	+	:
real:	A	B	C	D	E	F	G	H	I	J	K	L	M	N	O	P	Q	R	S	T	U	V	W	X	Y	Z

encode this: MY HANDWRITING IS ROTTEN.

decode this: ' + , + @ ? $ (− , ? (− ; . $ (! / ¼ $ (− , ? (

In Edgar Allan Poe's story "The Gold Bug," there is a random substitution cipher message, supposedly written by Captain Kidd, that tells where treasure is hidden. The message was written on parchment in invisible ink. The symbols used were a mixture of numbers and punctuation marks.

In Arthur Conan Doyle's story "The Adventures of the Dancing Men," Sherlock Holmes has to break a substitution cipher that uses stick figures for each letter of the alphabet.

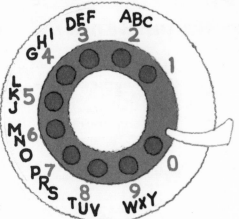

19 Telephone Cipher

A telephone dial makes a good starting point for a cipher—especially since there is usually one around to help in encoding and decoding.

On a telephone dial each number is put with a group of three letters. The numbers 1 and 0 have no letters with them, but to even things out, there are two letters, **Q** and **Z**, that are not on the dial.

To encode a message in the Telephone Cipher, let 1 stand for **Q** and 0 for **Z**. For the rest of the code, find the letter you need and write down the number of the group. If the letter is on the left of the group, put a dot to the left of the number. If the letter is on the right, put a slash mark to the right of the number. If the letter is in the middle, put a line over the top of the number. For example, .7=P 7̄=R 7/=S

---

encode this: STRAWBERRY ICE CREAM IS BEST.

decode this: 4/ 5/4/5̄3 .6.2.75/3̄ .9.25/6̄8.8

To cause confusion if your message should fall into the wrong hands, reverse the order of the numbers on the telephone dial. Draw a diagram with the 1 where the 0 is, the 2 where the 9 is, and so on around the dial. Just make sure your partner knows what the method is.

20 The Skytale

A Skytale is a cylinder around which a strip of paper can be wrapped in a spiral. After the paper is wrapped, a message is written across one side of the cylinder. The cylinder is then turned and the message is continued until it is finished. When the paper is unwrapped, the letters of the message are scrambled. The message cannot be read until the paper is wrapped over a Skytale of the same size.

Pencils and one-half inch by twelve inch strips of paper are good for learning how to use a Skytale. Pencils are too thin, however, for sending long messages and too common for sending secret messages. Try to find something to use as a Skytale that is at least an inch thick. Some suggestions are the cardboard tubes from inside rolls of paper, empty cans, flashlights, or just paper rolled to a predecided thickness. Just make sure that both you and your partner have Skytales the same size.

Adding-machine paper, which can be bought at a stationery store, is a good size for Skytale paper. Newspaper, cut into strips, is even better. If you print lightly, your message won't even be seen next to the type—except by your partner, who will know how to look for it.

Skytales were first used by the Greeks in about 500 B.C. Greek rulers sent Skytale messages to commanders during battles.

21 The Code Wheel

Cut two circles out of cardboard, one a little smaller than the other. Around the rim of the smaller wheel, print the alphabet in the regular order. Draw lines between the letters and make sure that each letter takes up the same amount of space. This smaller wheel will be your real alphabet.

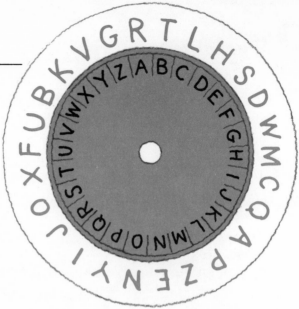

With a paper fastener, fasten the real alphabet wheel, through its center, to the center of the larger wheel. Along the rim of the larger wheel, opposite the letters of the real alphabet, print the letters of the cipher alphabet. The cipher alphabet can either be printed in regular or random order. Here it is printed in random order.

To use the wheel to send a message in code, first decide on a key letter. Here the key letter is **R.** Turn the wheels until the key letter on the outside wheel is lined up with the **A** on the inside wheel. Keep the wheels in that position. For each letter in your message, find the letter on the inside wheel (the real alphabet) and copy down the letter opposite it on the outside wheel (the cipher alphabet). You and your partner must both have identical wheels—and know the key letter.

A Code Wheel can be used to encode and decode many different substitution ciphers quickly. This wheel is set up to use with alphabet substitution ciphers, but the same type of wheel can be used for number and symbol substitution ciphers.

The Code Wheel was invented in the fifteenth century by an Italian architect— Leon Battista Alberti.

22 The Zigzag Strip

Write the alphabet in a column, but in any order at all, on a strip of paper. On the right hand edge of the strip, cut three or four notches. And that's your Zigzag Strip Key—you can hide it almost anywhere. Your partner will need one just like it.

To encipher a message with the Zigzag Strip Key, put the key against the left hand edge of a piece of paper. Lined paper, turned sideways, is good to use the first few times for practice. Mark notches on the message paper in the same places as the notches on the key. Put a pencil dot or a pin prick on the line nearest the first letter in the message. A little farther to the right, put another dot even with the next letter of the message…and go on until the message is finished. You don't need to draw lines between letter/dots, since the message moves from left to right, but you can if you want to make the dots look like part of a picture.

To decipher a message, match the key notches with the message notches and read from left to right.

A piece of wrapping paper, with a design on it, is especially good for sending pin-prick messages. The message will not be noticed on the design side, but it will be seen easily on the plain side.

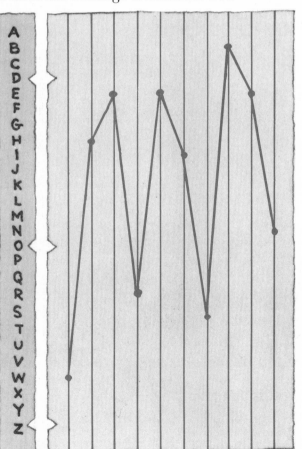

Hobos often left signs around to tell others, in a secret way, what sort of greeting could be expected. The code messages were chalked on fence posts or sides of houses—to anyone who didn't know what they meant, they looked like kids' scribbling. Hobo signs might be handy at Halloween.

food

nice woman

mean man

don't give up

be strong

good place

fierce dog

be quiet

danger

women only

tell sad story

money

must work to eat

23 Invisible Inks

Drink Inks 1. The juice of a lemon, an orange, or a grapefruit. **2.** Two teaspoons of soda pop mixed with one teaspoon of water. **3.** Half a teaspoon of honey or sugar stirred into half a glass of water.

Stink Ink The juice of an onion. Peel the onion and grate it into a dish. Let it sit for about ten minutes. Some of the onion will become liquid—and a really good invisible ink. (Wash your hands after using so no one will smell that you are a spy.)

Write on soft, uncoated paper rather than shiny paper so that the ink will sink in and not be noticed when it dries. Use a tiny paint brush for a pen so that there are no pressure marks. You can also use a pen point or a toothpick, but write very lightly. Do not use a ballpoint or fountain pen. Messages can also be sent, with drink and stink inks, by brushing a bit of ink over "message" letters or words in the newspaper. Heat will make all of these invisible inks visible. Hold the message over a lightbulb, or electric toaster, or iron it lightly with a hot iron. Do not use matches or fire.

Cow Code Milk makes a good invisible ink. To send a milk message pour a little milk into a dish and use a tiny brush. Write on any thick, hard-surfaced paper; a file card is fine. When the milk dries the message will be invisible. To make it visible again, rub it with graphite powder. You can get graphite by scraping a lead pencil with a knife. Dip your fingers in the graphite powder and rub them over the milk message.

Present-day senders of secret messages can take advantage of modern discoveries. Whole paragraphs can be put on a piece of microfilm no bigger than the period at the end of this sentence.

24 Hidden Writing

Dry-up Writing Wet a piece of paper until it is damp. Put the wet paper up against a mirror or on a formica kitchen counter and cover it with a dry piece of paper. Write your message on the dry paper with a ballpoint pen or a very dull pencil. Press down hard as you write. Take the dry paper off and destroy it. As long as the message paper stays wet, you will be able to read it. When it dries, however, the message will become invisible. To make the message visible again, just wet the paper.

Cover-up Writing Write a message very lightly with a pencil. Crayon a picture or design over the message. All the receiver has to do to read the message is scrape off the crayon with a knife. If you use a lot of colors, always use the same color over the message. Tell your partner the "key" color to scrape off.

Fold-up Writing Fold a sheet of paper so that it has two or more vertical folds. Write your message so part of each word falls on a fold. Fill in the blanks between message words with dummy words. If you can, make the dummy words form a fake message. (That's really hard to do.)

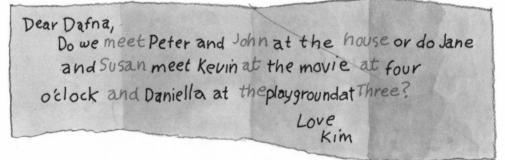

Secret messages have been sent sewn in the linings of coats, nailed between a shoe heel and sole, marked on belts, written on fans, and even tucked in a hollow tooth.

Cipher messages, in modern times, have been written on an envelope <u>under</u> the postage stamp.

25 The Morse Code

The Morse Code is really a substitution cipher. It was developed by Samuel Morse in 1832 to use over telegraph wires. A special type of code was needed for the telegraph since sounds, but not voices, could be sent over the wires. The Morse Code, which is still used today, is made up of sounds—combinations of clicks and rests—called dots and dashes. A dot is a click followed by a short rest; a dash is a click followed by a longer rest.

Morse was not trying to make a secret code. He wanted a code that could be used easily by many people. The Morse Code is arranged for the easiest possible use. Since **E** is the most frequently used letter in the alphabet, Morse gave it the shortest sound—a single dot. **T** is the next most frequently used letter and it has the next shortest sound—a single dash. The Morse Code was designed to be an "out loud" code, but when it is written out it looks like this:

A •—	H ••••	O ———	V •••—
B —•••	I ••	P •——•	W •——
C —•—•	J •———	Q ——•—	X —••—
D —••	K —•—	R •—•	Y —•——
E •	L •—••	S •••	Z ——••
F ••—•	M ——	T —	
G ——•	N —•	U ••—	

The Morse Code can be used as a "sound" code by tapping with pencils, fingers, or sticks, or by blowing on whistles. It can be a "sight" code used with flags or flashing lights. And, of course, it can be a written code.

encode this: YOUR FLASHLIGHT IS GETTING DIM.

decode this: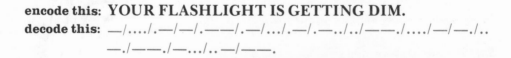

Simple-sounding tunes can be used to encipher and send secret messages. The order of notes, the rhythm of the song, and any accompanying sounds can each stand for a different letter. A girl walking down the street humming a tune could really be telling an agent to be ready to leave at noon. A young boy whistling and clapping his hands as he plays in the woods may be warning his friends that an enemy is near.

Remember, when sounds are used to stand for whole words, phrases, or sentences, they are part of a code rather than a cipher.

Sound codes have been used by many peoples in many countries. Africans and American Indians of many tribes have used drums to send messages, secret or not. And some Indian tribes used bird calls and other animal sounds to send messages.

There have been experiments using telepaths to send silent secret messages to other telepaths. It doesn't always work...and even when it does, no one is sure how to stop "enemy" telepaths from listening in.

In World War II, Navaho Indians called messages and instructions across the battlefield in their own language. The enemy never understood what was said.

26 Pig Latin

There are really only three rules for speaking Pig Latin.

Rule 1: When a word begins with a vowel (a,e,i,o,u) add the three letters **WAY** to the end of the word.

I**WAY**   AM**WAY**   AWAY**WAY**   IN**WAY**   IOWA**WAY**

Rule 2: When a word begins with a single consonant (any letter except a,e,i,o,u) take the first letter of the word and put it at the end of the word—then add the two letters **AY**.

IVEG**AY**   ISAL**AY**   ERH**AY**   OOKB**AY**   ACKB**AY**

Rule 3: When a word begins with a group of two or more consonants (such as th, ch, br, pl, sc, sch, thr) move the whole group of letters to the end of the word—then add the two letters **AY**.

ATTH**AY**   INKERST**AY**   IKESSTR**AY**   ILDRENCH**AY**

---

encode this: CHICKENS CANNOT SPEAK PIG LATIN AT ALL.
decode this: OOTAY UCHMAY IGPAY ATINLAY AKESMAY AWAY OGHAY OFWAY OUYAY

Another language is really a code if you and your partner know it and no one else does. Does someone in your family come from another country or speak another language? Ask to learn a few important words in that language.

36

Cipher Breaking

Learning to break even slightly difficult ciphers is very hard. Before computers came to the rescue, cryptanalysts—experts on breaking ciphers—would work for days, months, or even years on a single message.

There are some facts about the use of letters in the English language, however, that might help you break the cipher in captured messages.

1. **E** is the letter used most often. In every 1,000 words, **E** will appear 591 times, or 126 times in every 1,000 letters.
2. **T,O,A,** and **N,** in that order, are the most common letters after **E.**
3. **T** is the most common letter at the beginning of a word.
4. **E** is the most common letter at the end of a word.
5. **A** and **I** are the only single-letter words in English, although **O** is sometimes used.
6. **OF, TO,** and **IN,** in that order, are the most frequent two-letter words.
7. **LL,EE,OO,TT,FF,RR,NN,PP,** and **CC,** in that order, are the most common double letters.
8. **TH, HE, AN, RE, ER,** and **IN,** in that order, are the most frequent two-letter combinations.
9. **N** is the consonant that most often follows a vowel.
10. **THE** and **AND,** in that order, are the most frequent three-letter words.
11. **THE, ING, AND, ION,** and **ENT,** in that order, are the most frequent three-letter combinations.
12. **THAT** is the most frequent four-letter word.

And, of course, don't forget that **Q** is always followed by **U.**

Do these rules prove true on this page?

One cryptanalyst worked for three years to break a cipher a famous man had used in writing his diary. He was probably a bit upset when a complete key to the cipher was found—after he had finished.

For practice, decode the riddle answers and encode the riddle questions.
The cipher number and any necessary hints are given after the riddle answer.

1

What are five animals in the bear family?

SRAE BYB ABE ERHTD
NARA EBAP POPR AEBA MAM (cipher 3)

2

Which is heavier, a half moon or a full moon?

AAFO NEAS AULO NSIH
EHLMOB CUEF LMOI LGTR
(cipher 4)

3

Why did the liar keep his word?

YBZXRPB KL LKB TLRIA QXHB FQ
(cipher 6)

4

Why does the ocean roar?

232| .287|3 4|.8 4.27| 23.3
4|6 4.87|23.3
4/6 4.87|23.3
(cipher 19)

5

When is a piece of wood like a king?

JURA UH TH X ILUNI
(cipher 13)

6

Who earns a living without doing a day's work?

1 14-9-7-8-20 23-1-20-3-8-13-1-14
(cipher 10)

7

What did the nasty frog say to the nastier frog?

⌐ ⊓⊔┌⊏ ⊽⊔⊓ ⌐⊔⊔⌐⊳
(cipher 16)

8

What is always coming but never arrives?

(cipher 14)

9

How do trains hear?
,0(!)¼0 ,0?-(?/¼-/??(;
(cipher 18)

10

Why can't a train sit down?
**BSANE HDSEE CIAEI
NRTTA UHEBD**
(cipher 5, 5x5, pathway 1)

Answers:
1. Mama bear, poppa bear, and three baby bears. **2.** A half moon because a full moon is lighter. **3.** Because no one would take it. **4.** Because it has crabs in its bed. **5.** When it is a ruler. **6.** A night watchman. **7.** I hope you croak. **8.** Tomorrow. **9.** Through their engineers. **10.** Because it has a tender behind.

What did Paul Revere say at the end of his ride?

•— •••• ——— •—

Paul Revere's lantern signals—one if by land, two if by sea—
were a secret warning code.

GSV VMW